how to draw
amazing nature

**3dtotal
KIDS**

Email: publishing@3dtotal.com
Website: www.3dtotal.com

How to Draw Amazing Nature © 2023, 3dtotal Publishing. All rights reserved. No part of this book can be reproduced in any form or by any means, without the prior written consent of the publisher.

First published in the United Kingdom, 2023, by 3dtotal Kids, an imprint of 3dtotal Publishing.

Address: 3dtotal.com Ltd, 29 Foregate Street, Worcester, WR1 1DS, United Kingdom.

Soft cover ISBN: 978-1-912843-76-3
Printed and bound in China
by C&C Offset Printing Co., Ltd

Written & illustrated by Erin Hunting

Editor: Marisa Lewis
Designer: Fiona Tarbet
Lead Editor: Samantha Rigby
Lead Designer: Joseph Cartwright
Studio Manager: Simon Morse
Managing Director: Tom Greenway

At 3dtotal Publishing we give 50% of our net profits to charities that help people, animals, and our planet. We also plant one tree for every book we sell.

Erin Hunting is a Melbourne-based illustrator and character designer who loves to create drawings for picture books and comics.

erinhunting.com

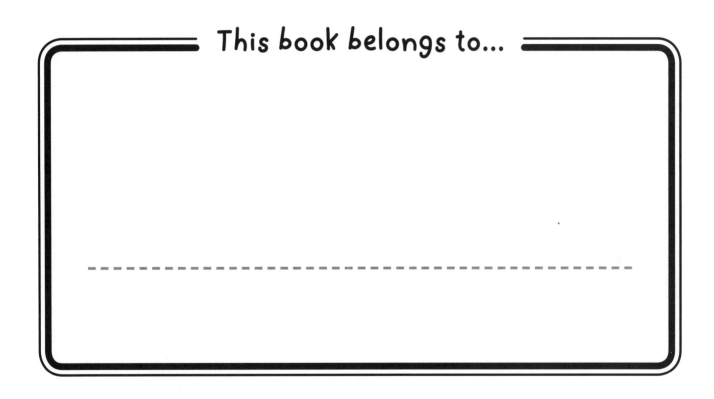

This book belongs to...

All you'll need is something to draw with:

pens crayons pencils markers

Whatever you like!

And also paper!

It can be loose or in a sketchbook:

So come on, let's have some fun!

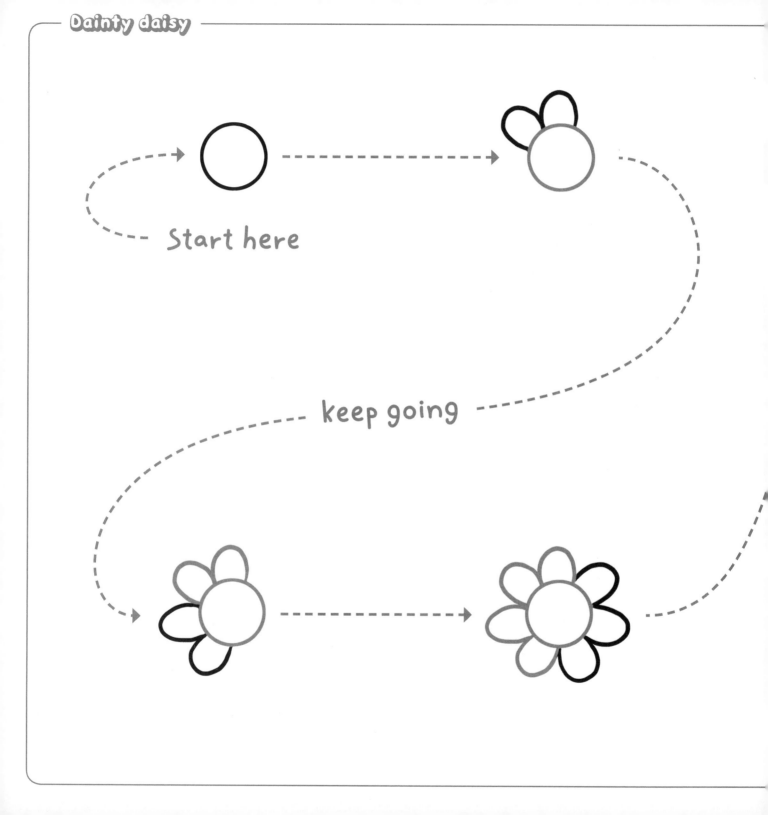

Start here

keep going

nearly there

All
done!

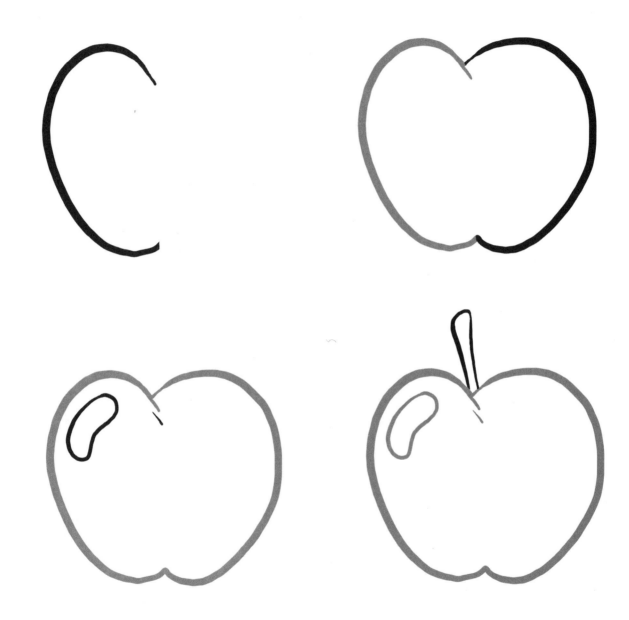

Rain clouds

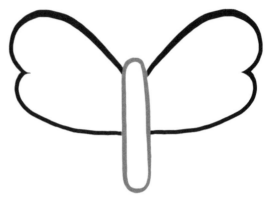

Tall tree

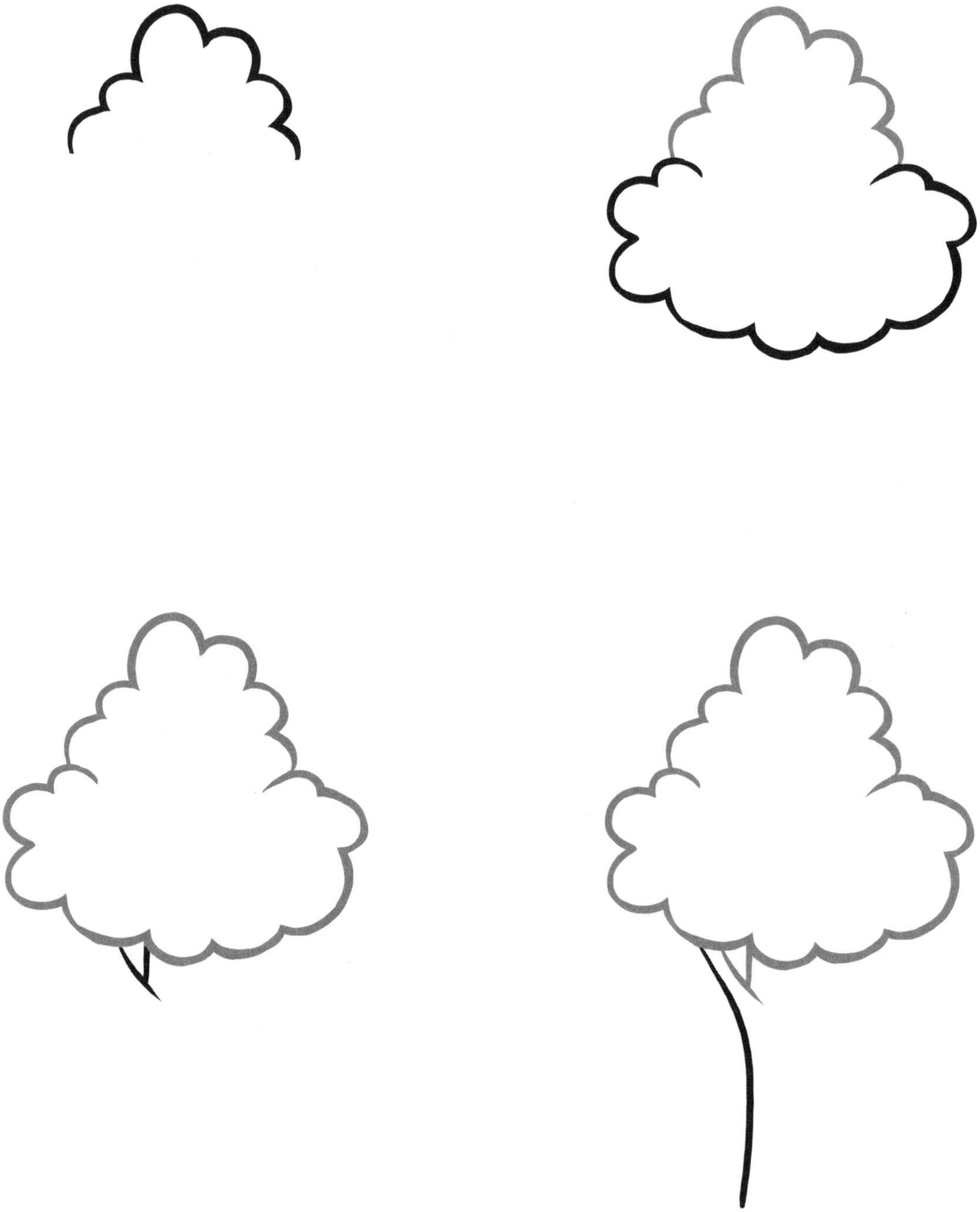

Toadstools

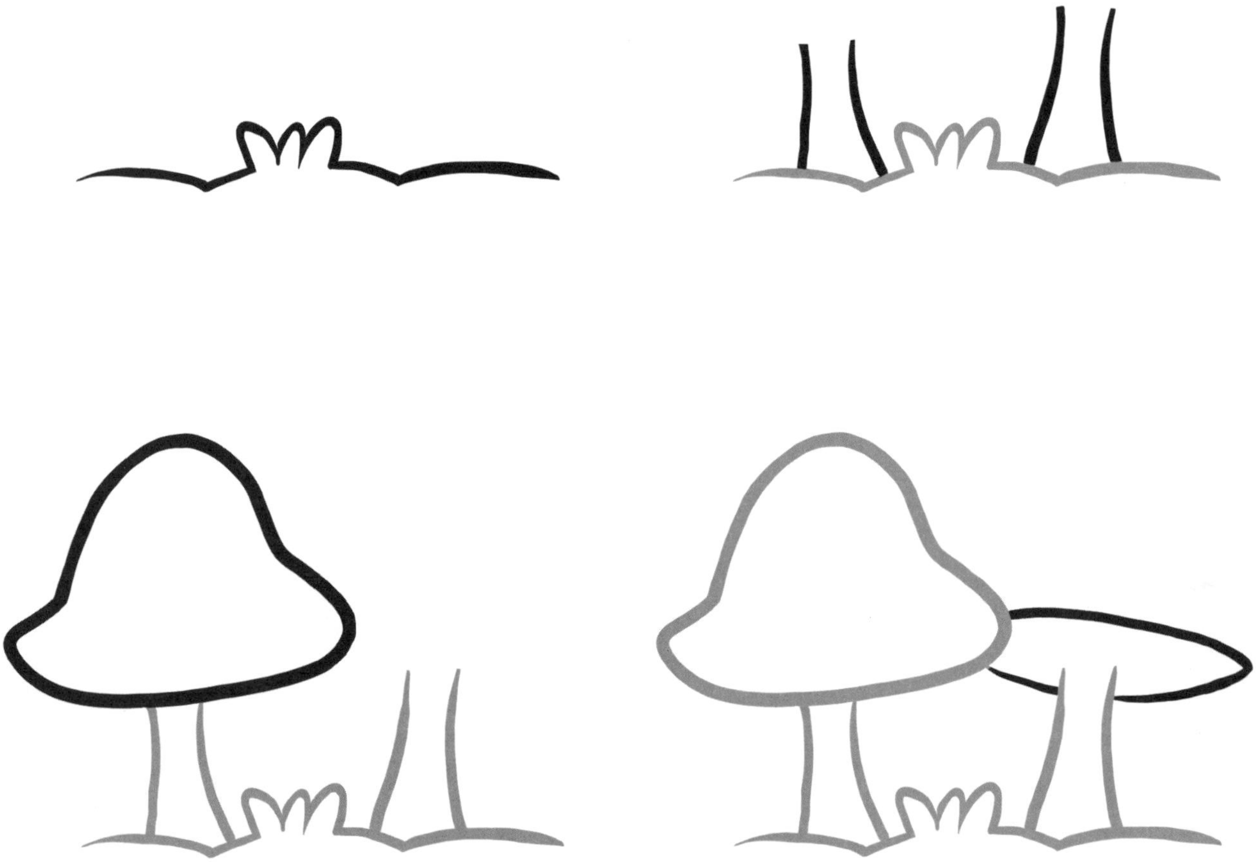

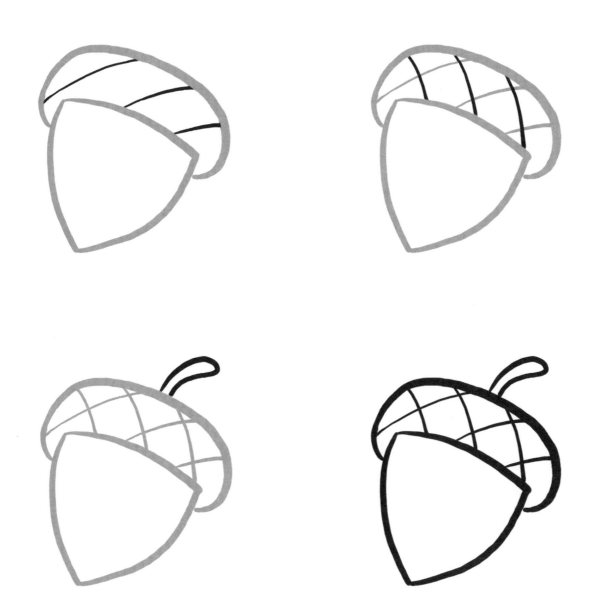

Have you ever noticed how many different shapes of leaves there are?

Try drawing some!

Shading with lines is called 'hatching'.

Shading with dots is called 'stippling'.

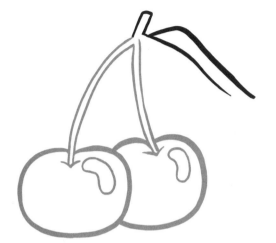

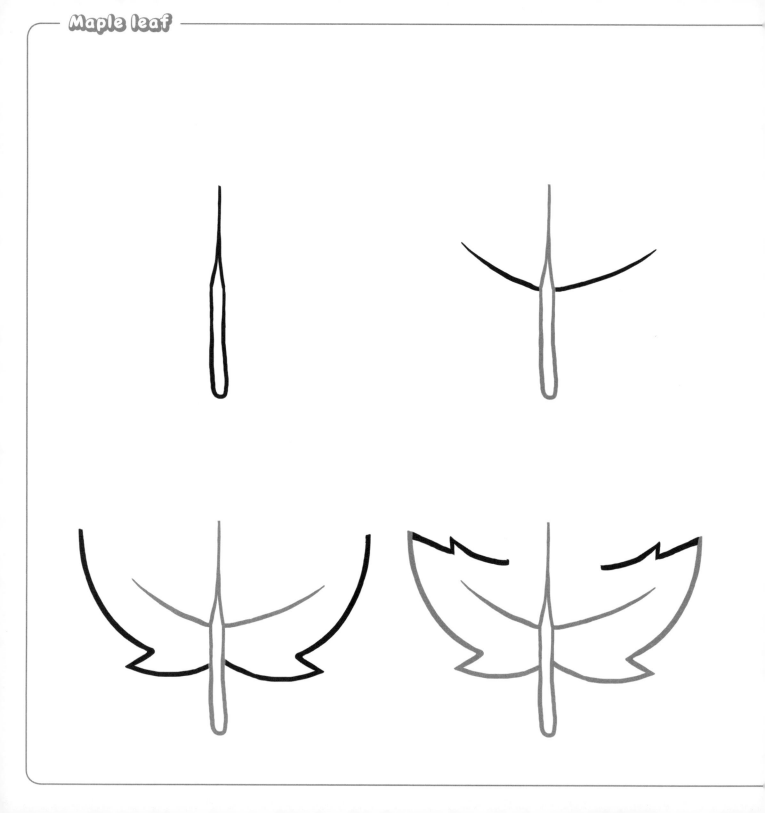

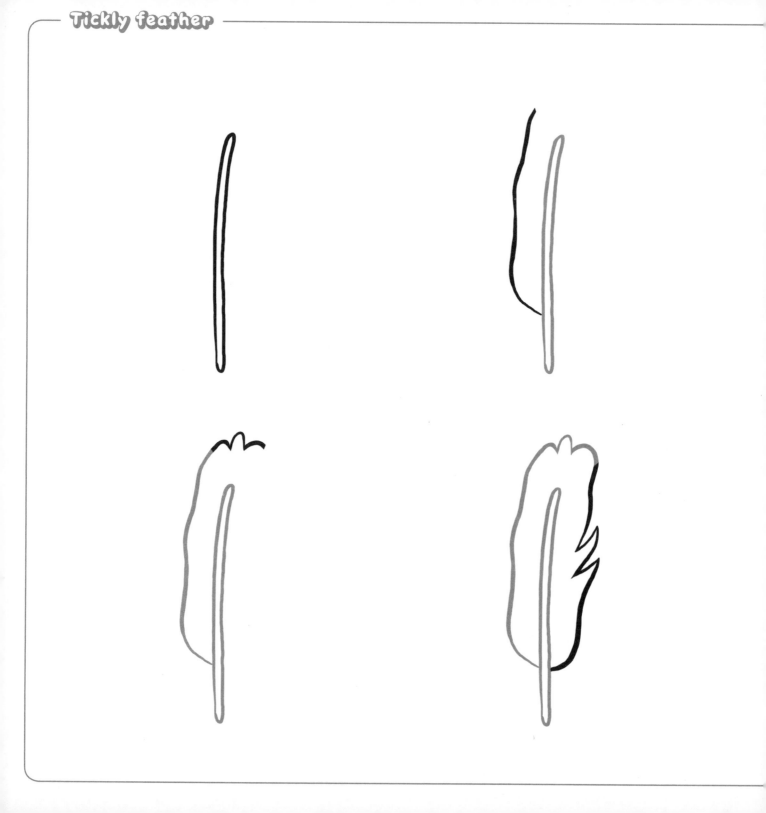

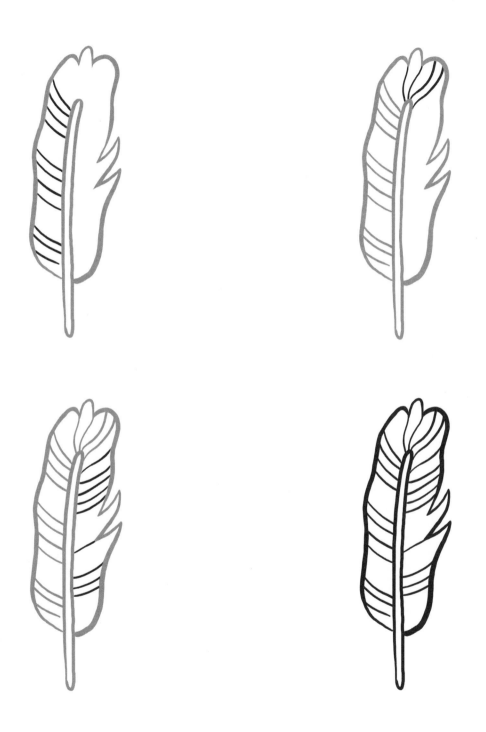

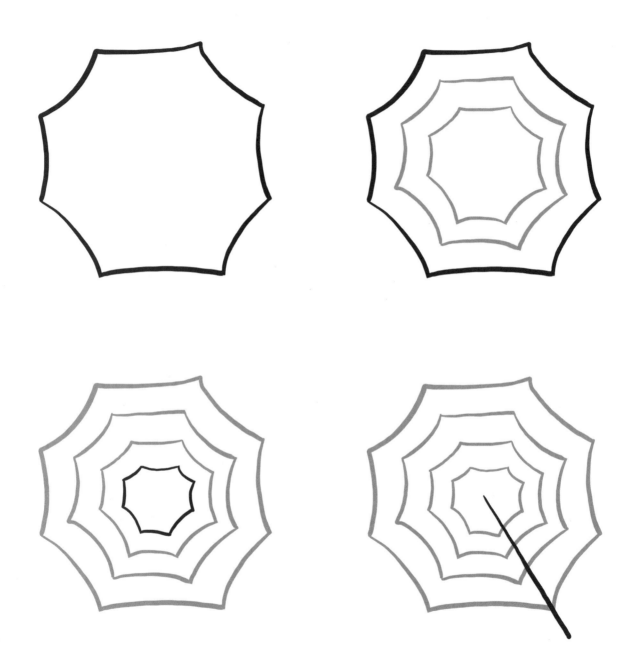

Slice of watermelon

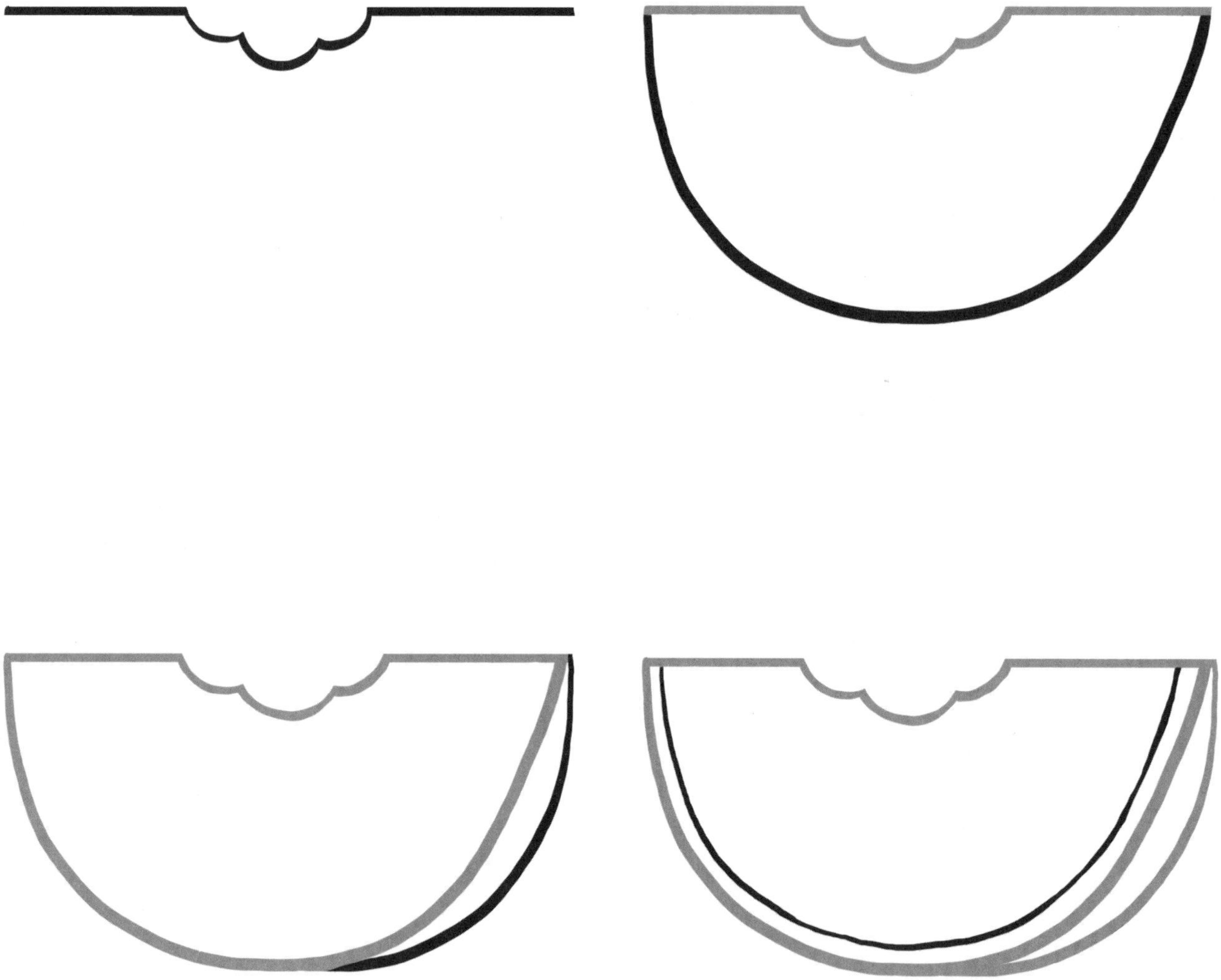

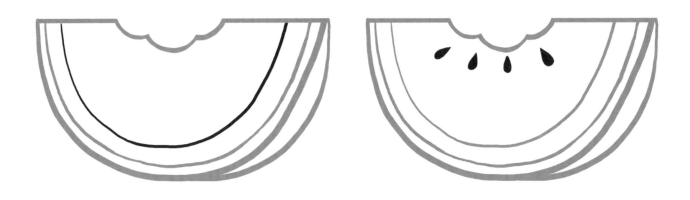

To show light and shade, imagine a light source
(like the sun) shining on the object:

The shadow would fall furthest
away from the sun.

Here are some more examples!

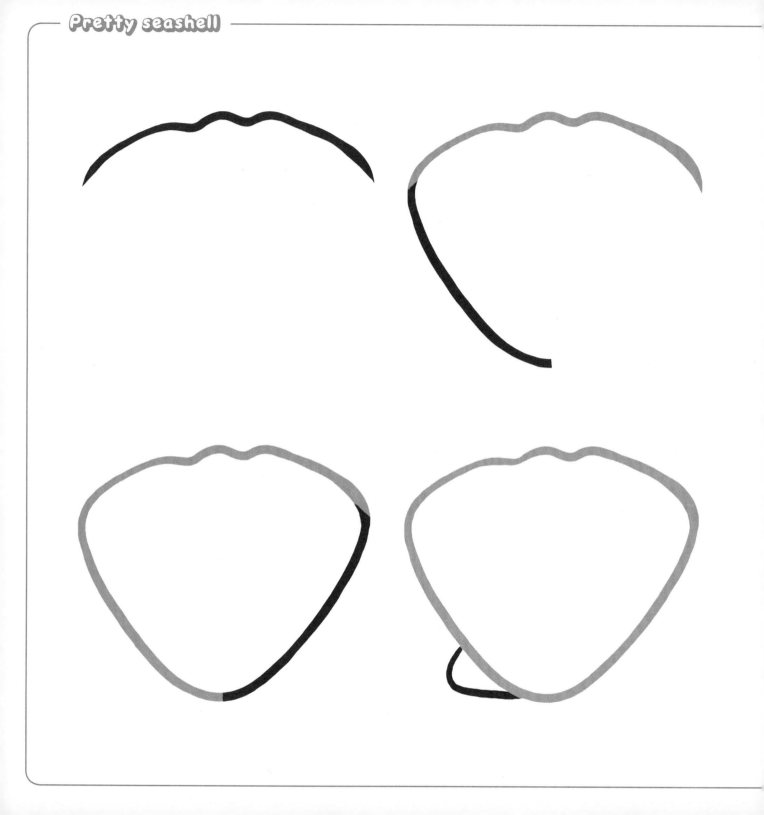

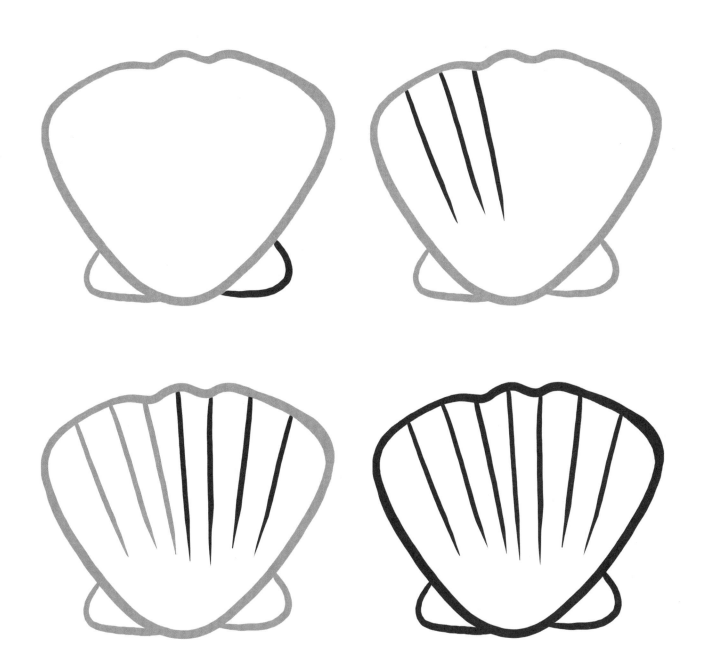

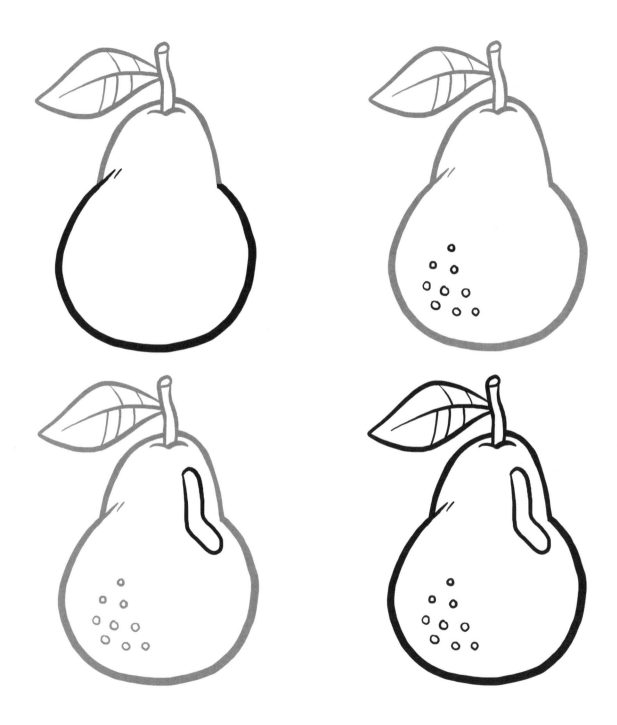

Busy beehive

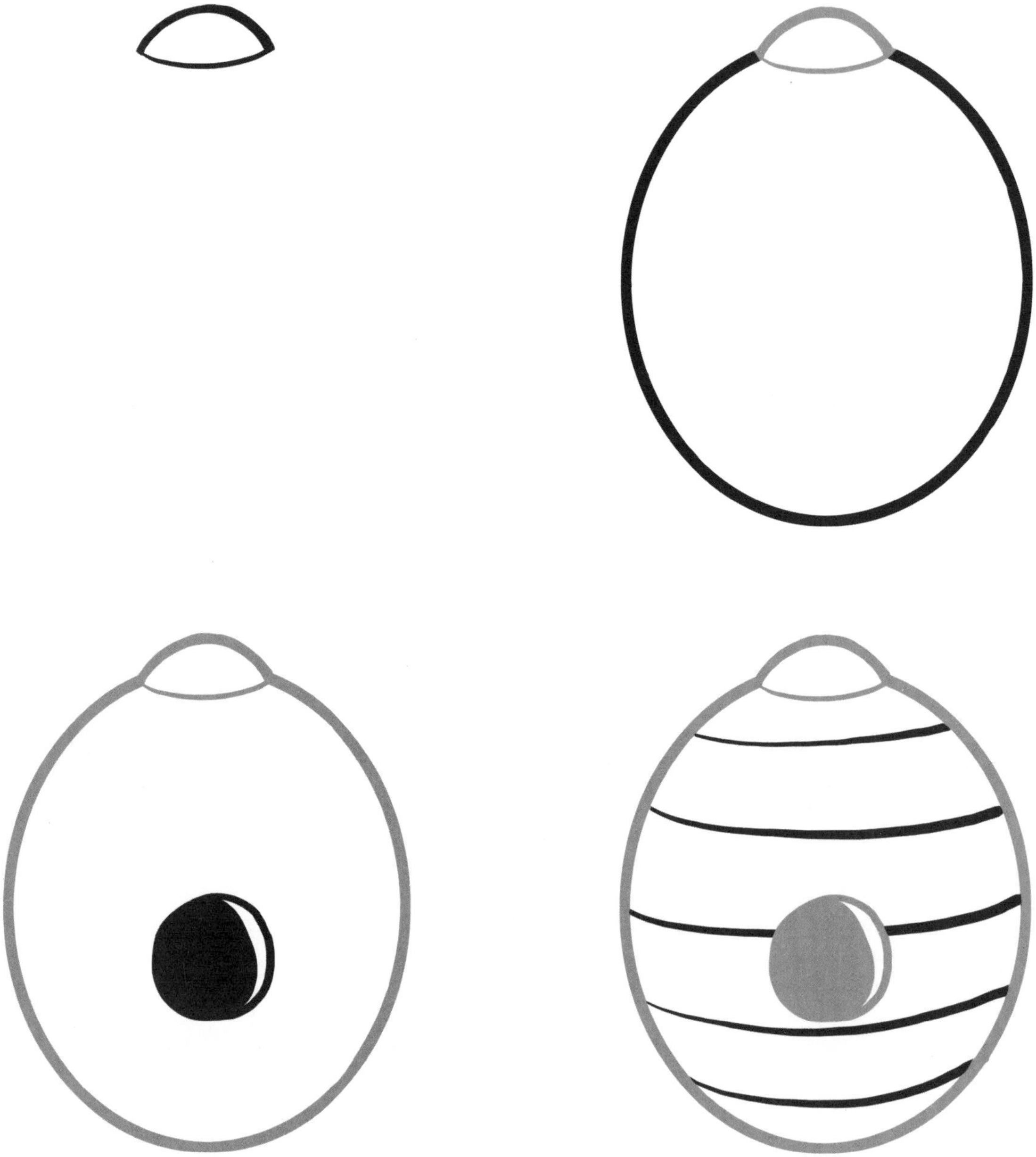

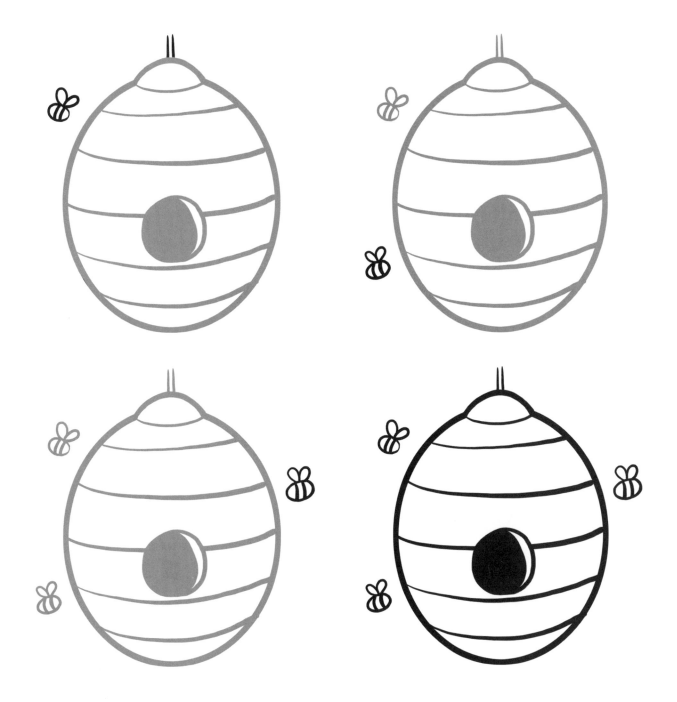

Potted plant

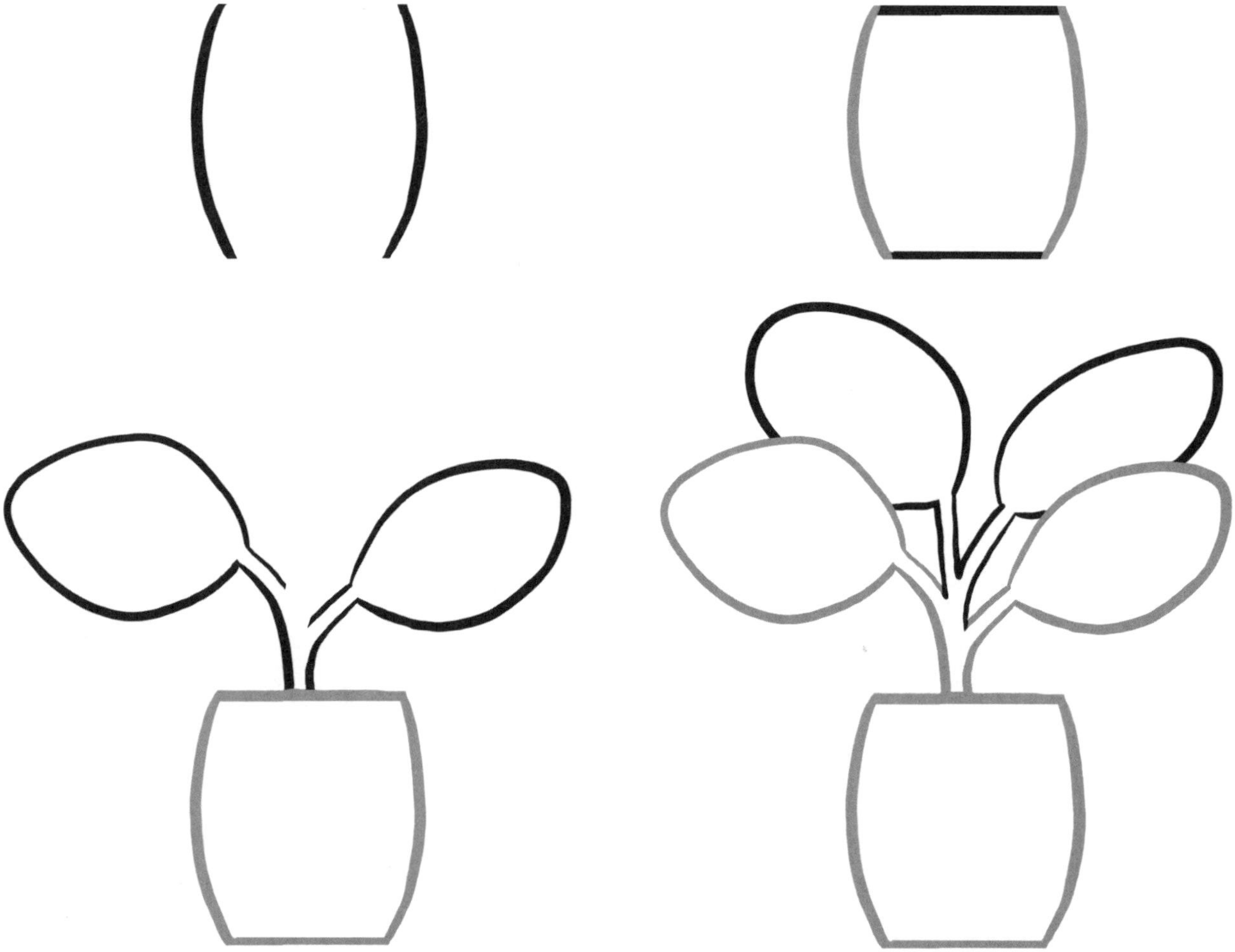

Campfire

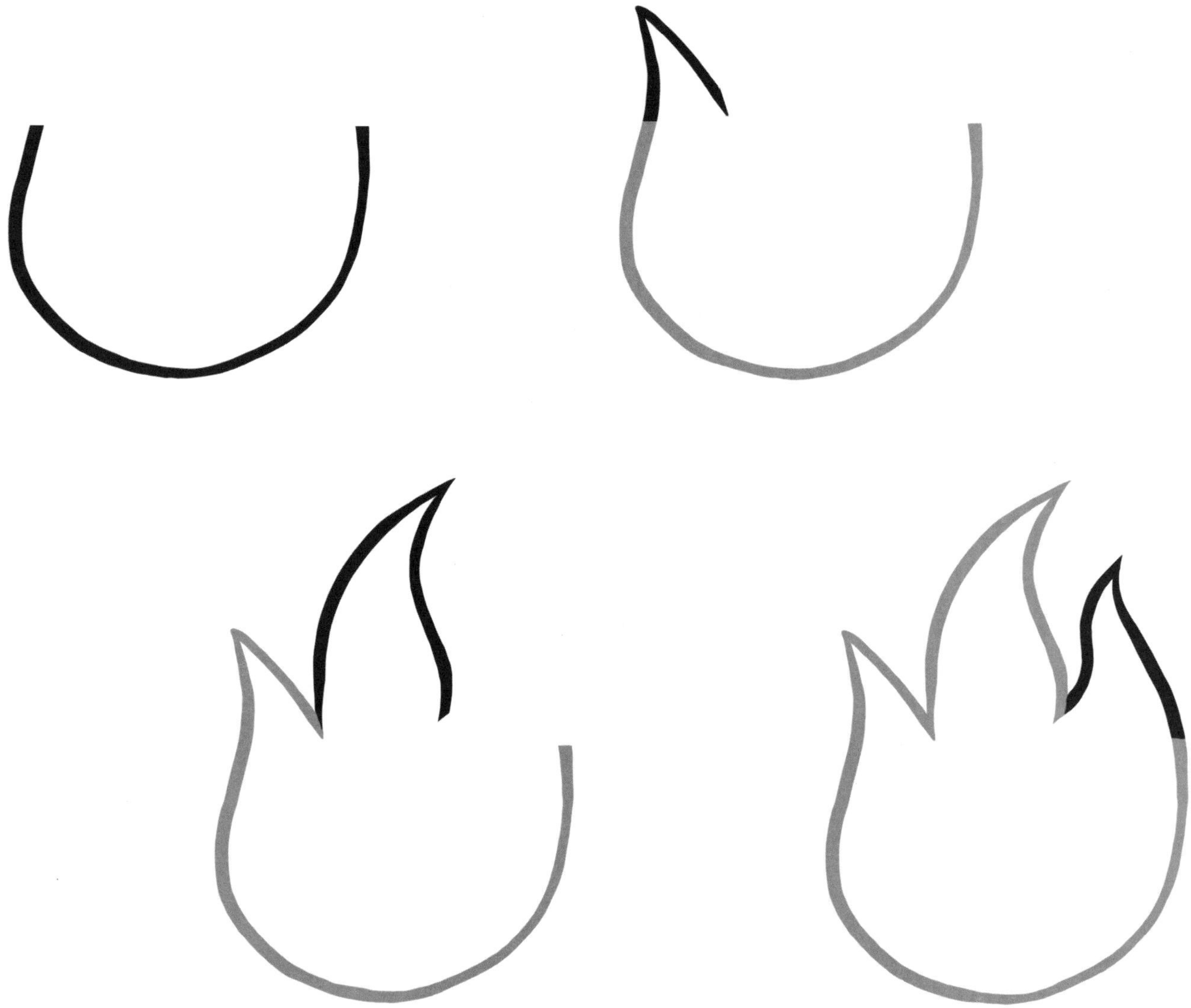

There are a lot of different tree types and shapes as well!

cherry blossom

stump

oak

chestnut

autumn

apple

palm

pine

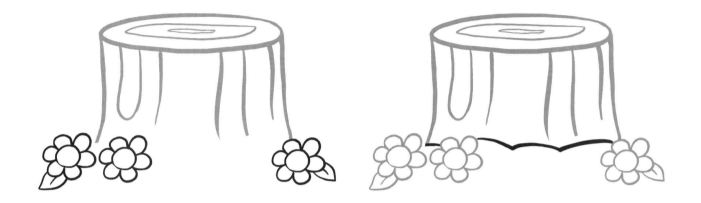

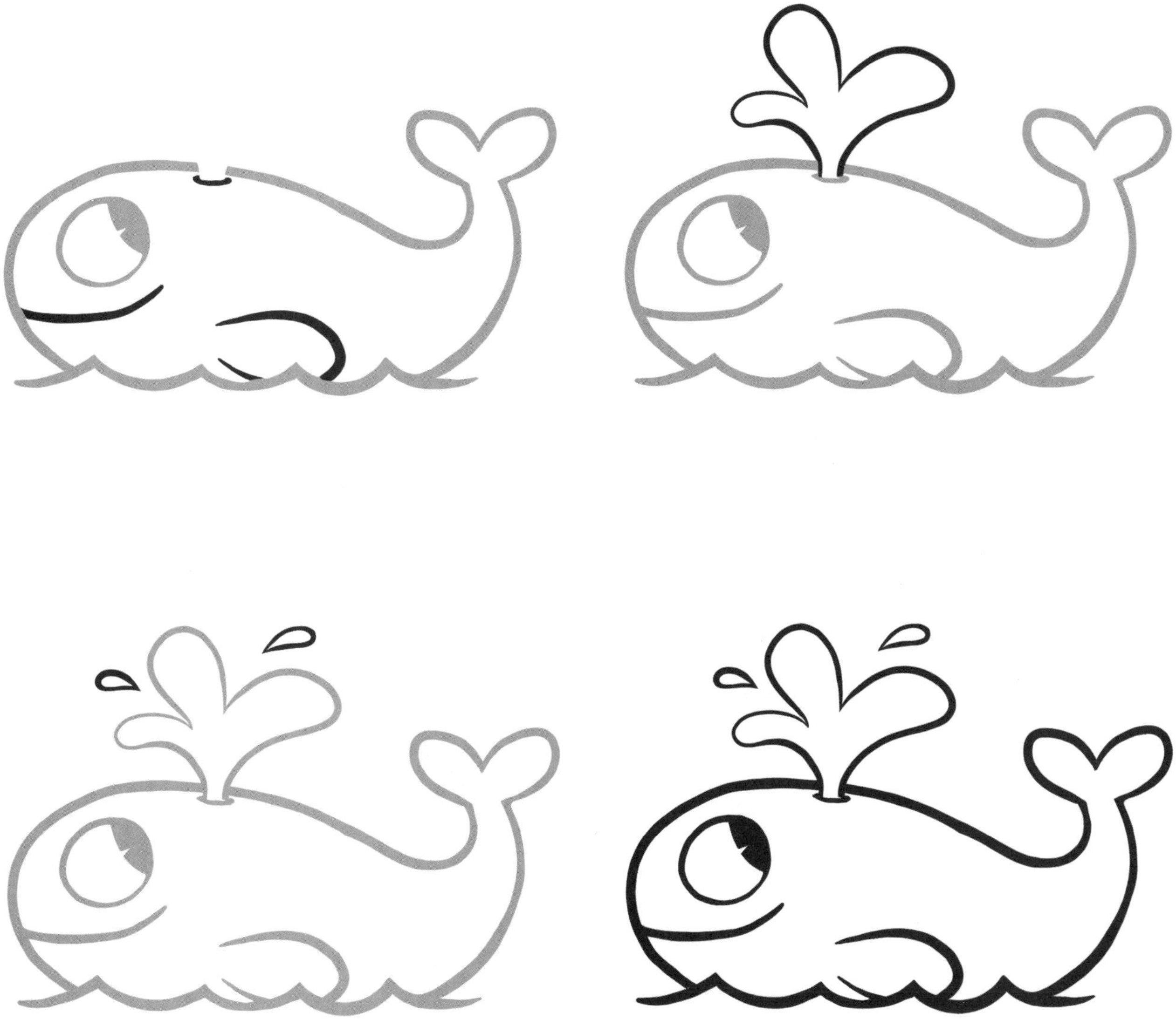

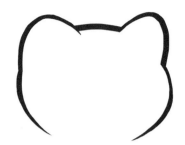

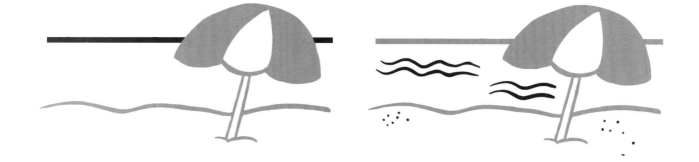

Crunchy carrot

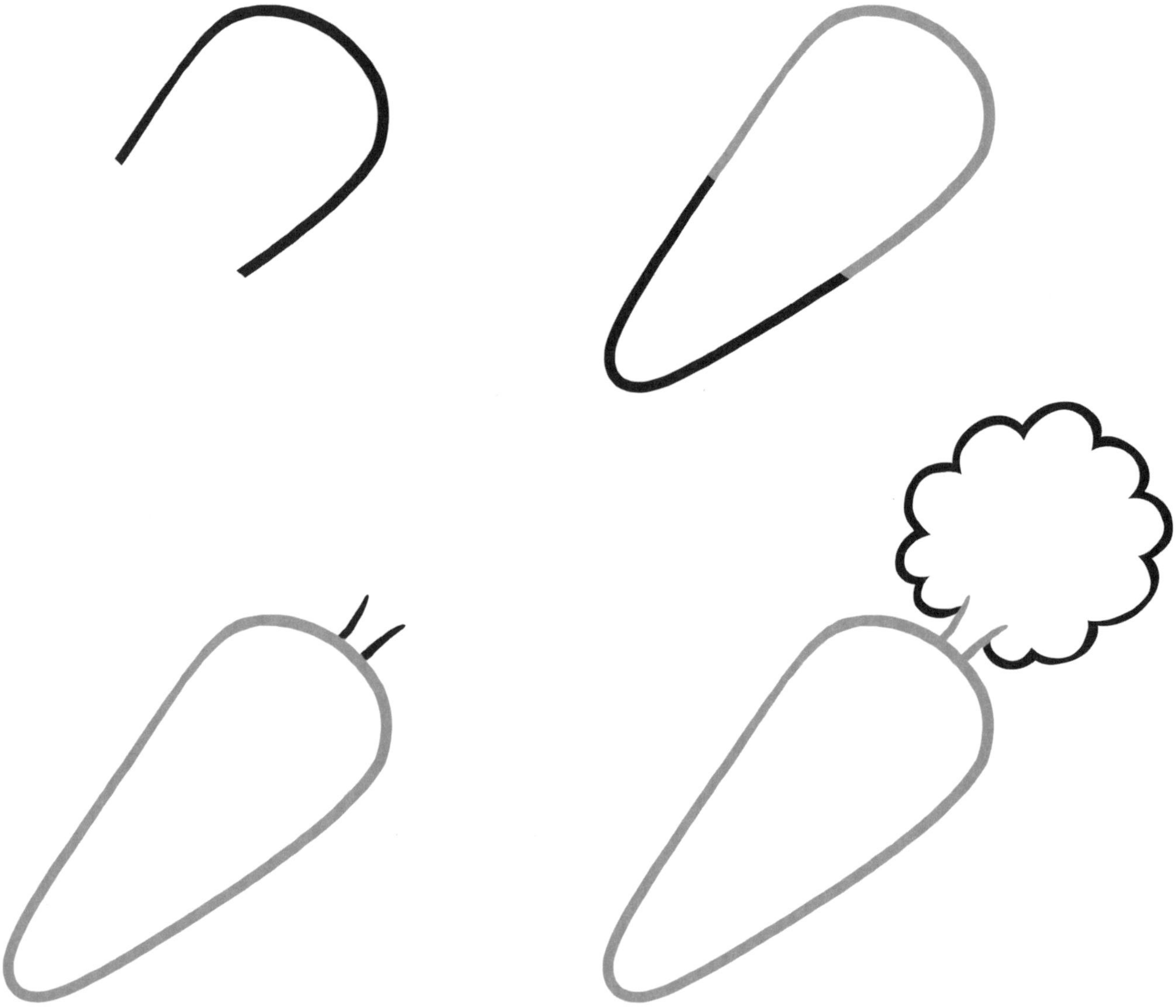

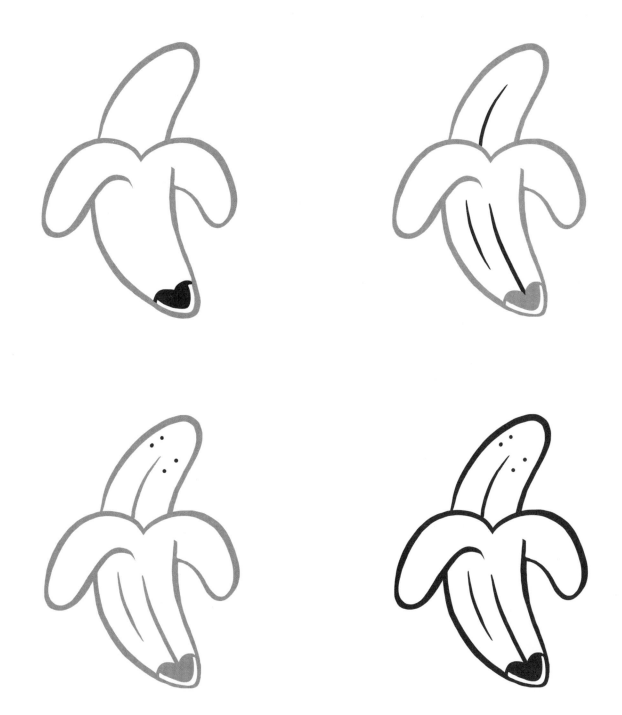

Spiky cactus

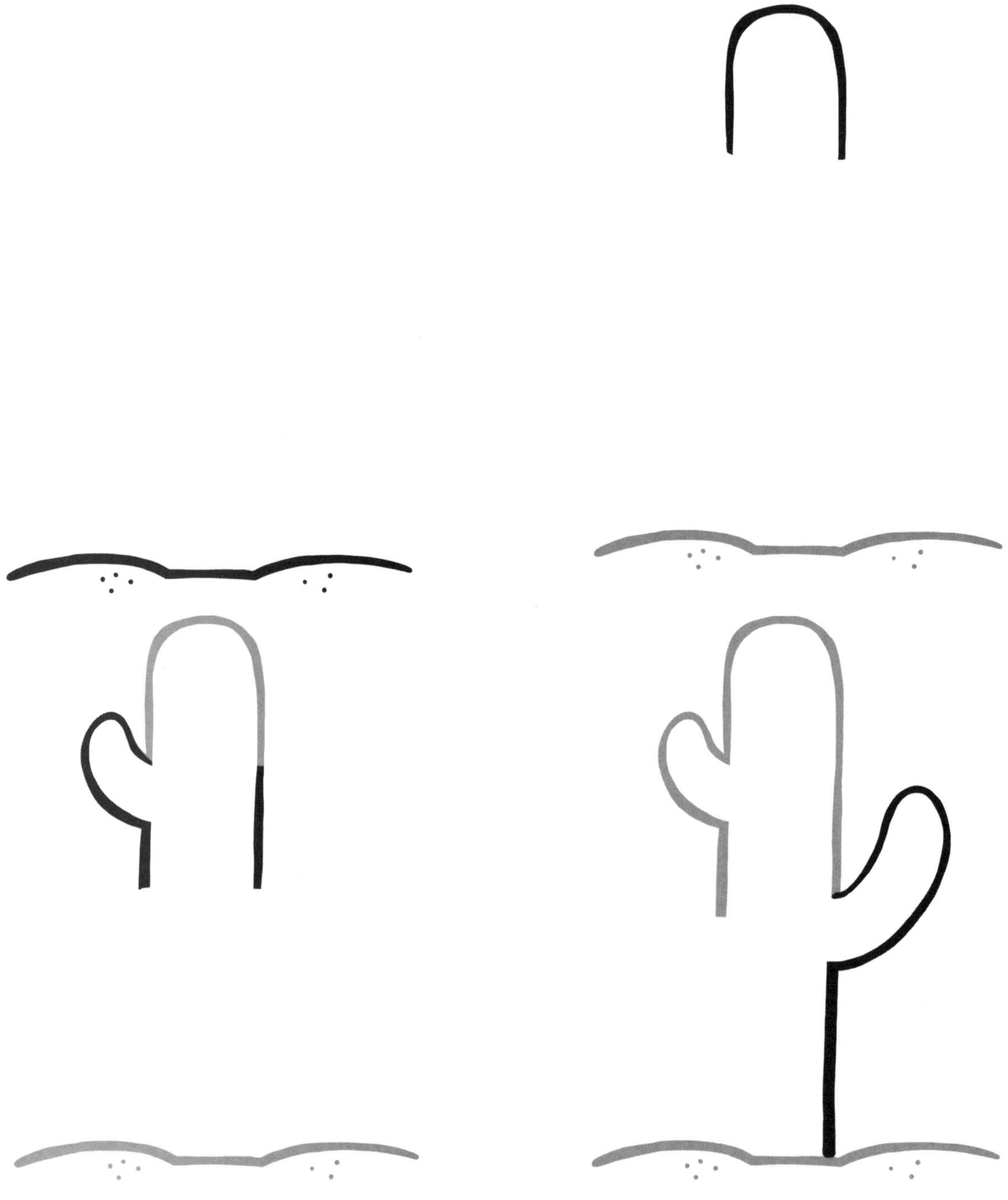

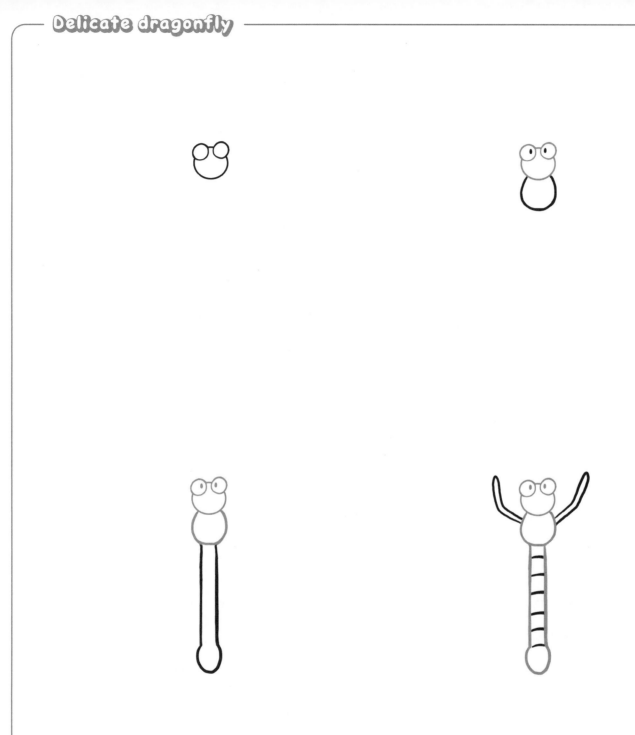

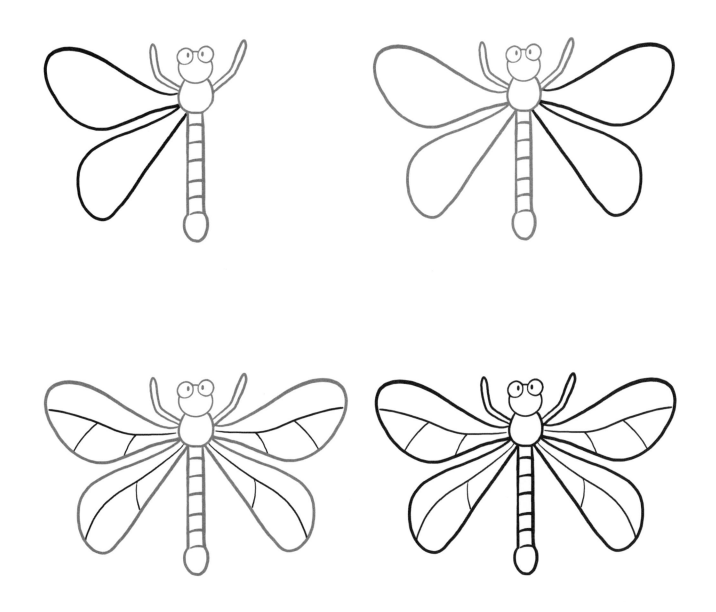

Erupting volcano

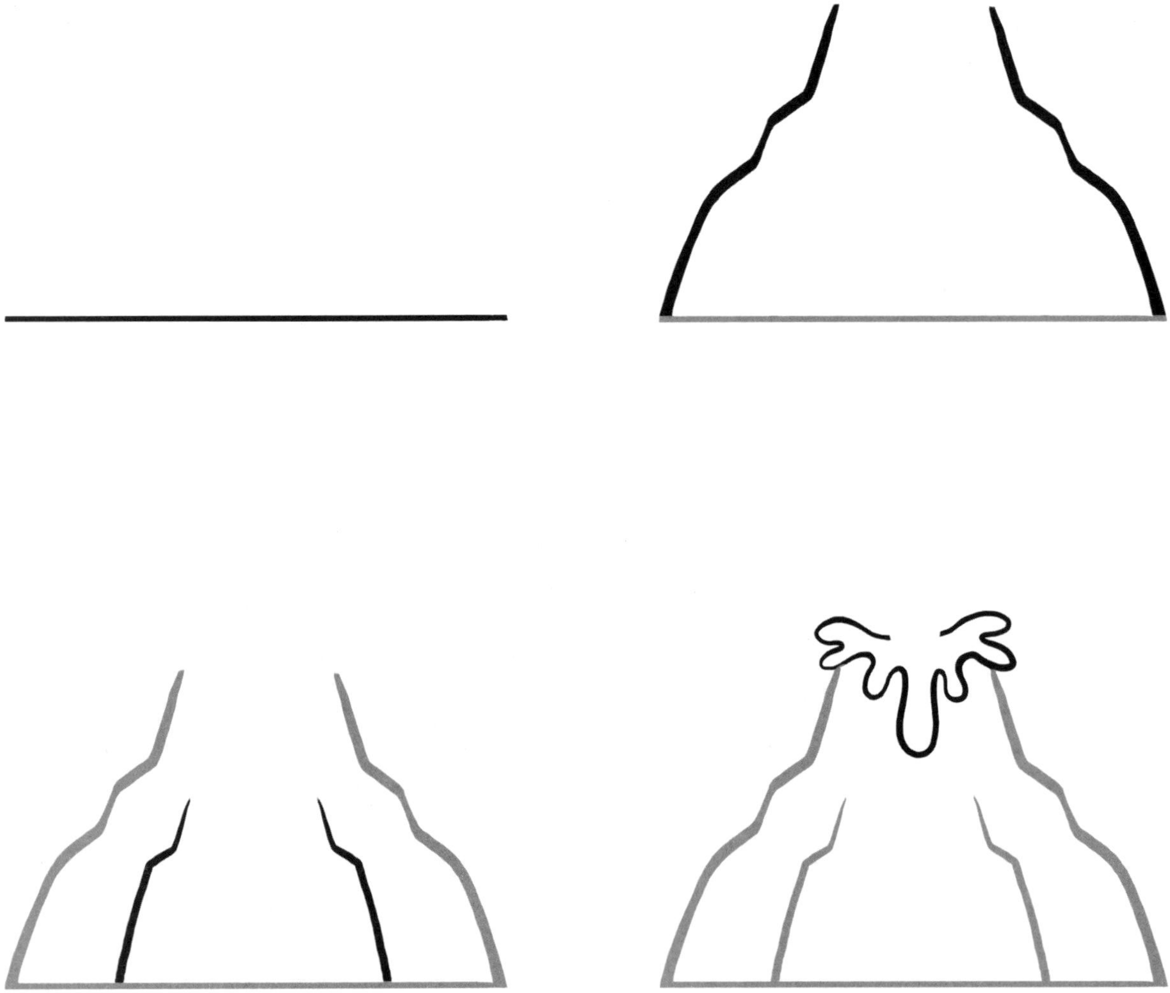

Many animals have unique fur markings, like these cats:

Can you remember and draw different
markings for wild animals too?

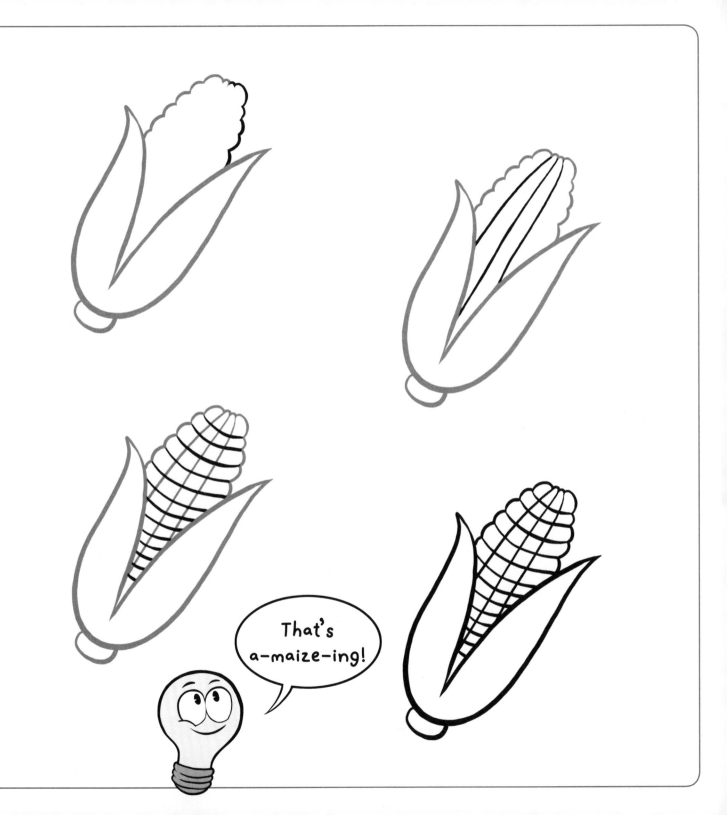

That's a-maize-ing!

Birds in their nest

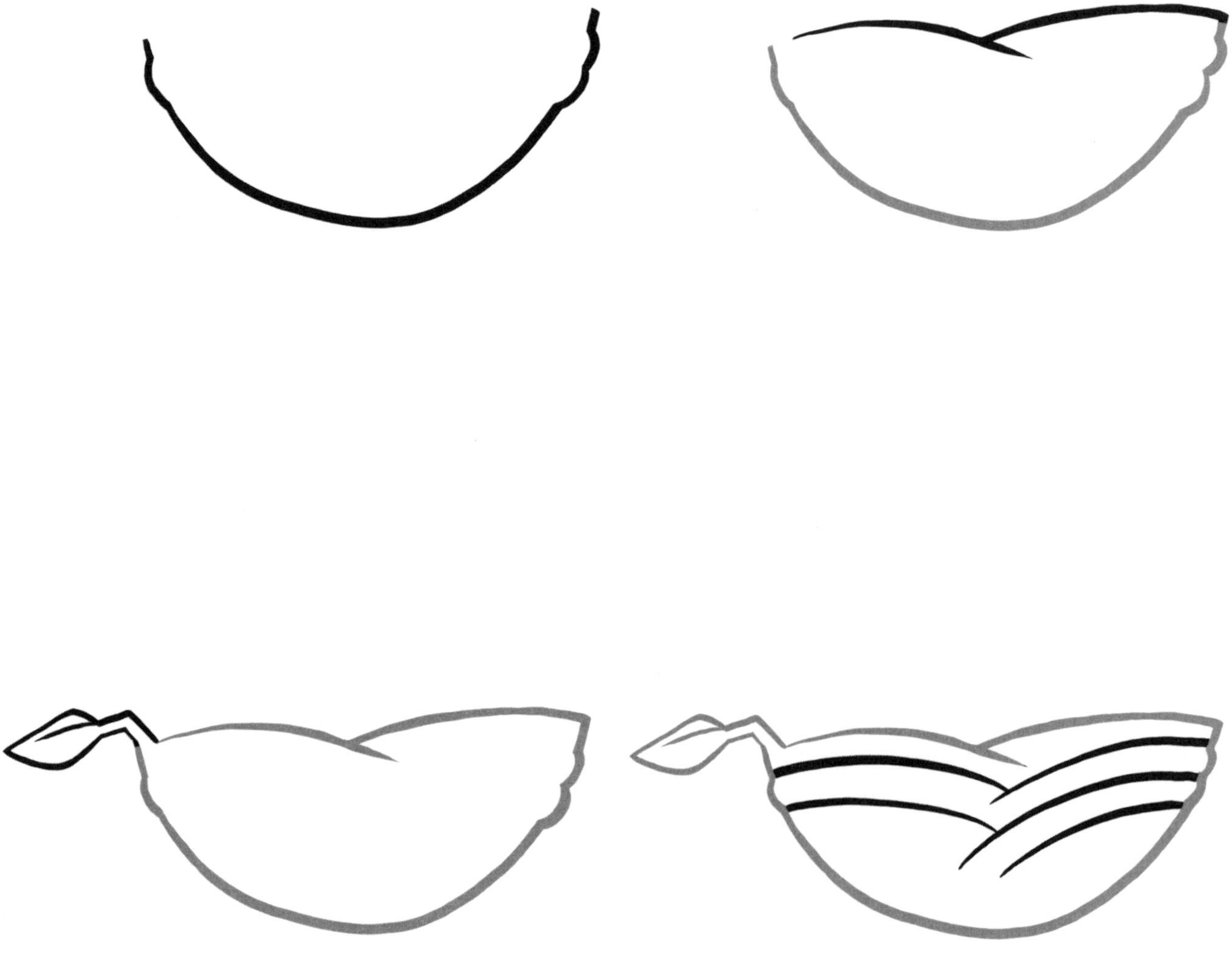

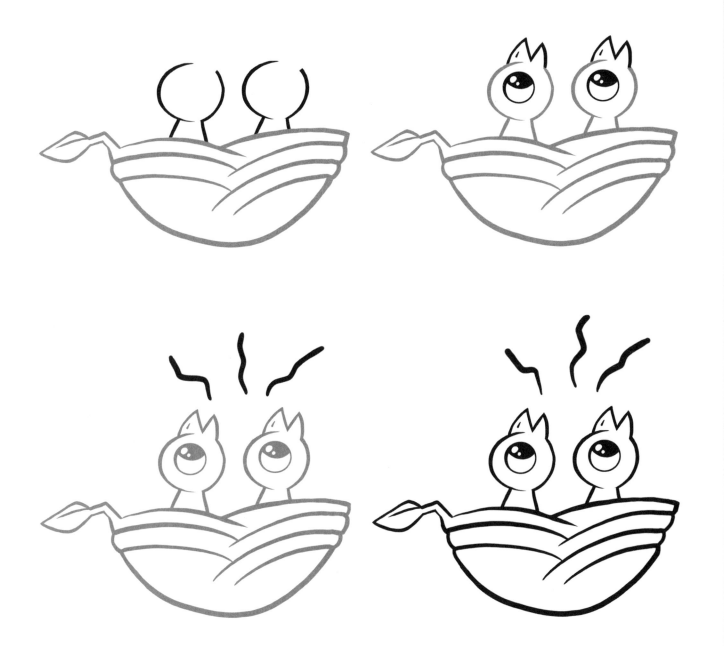

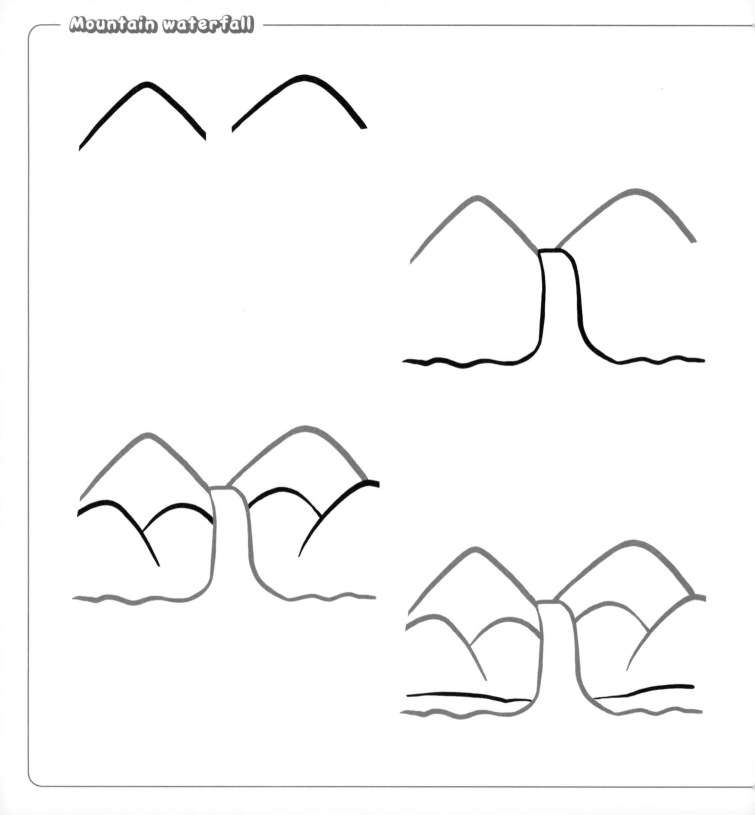

Ocean wave

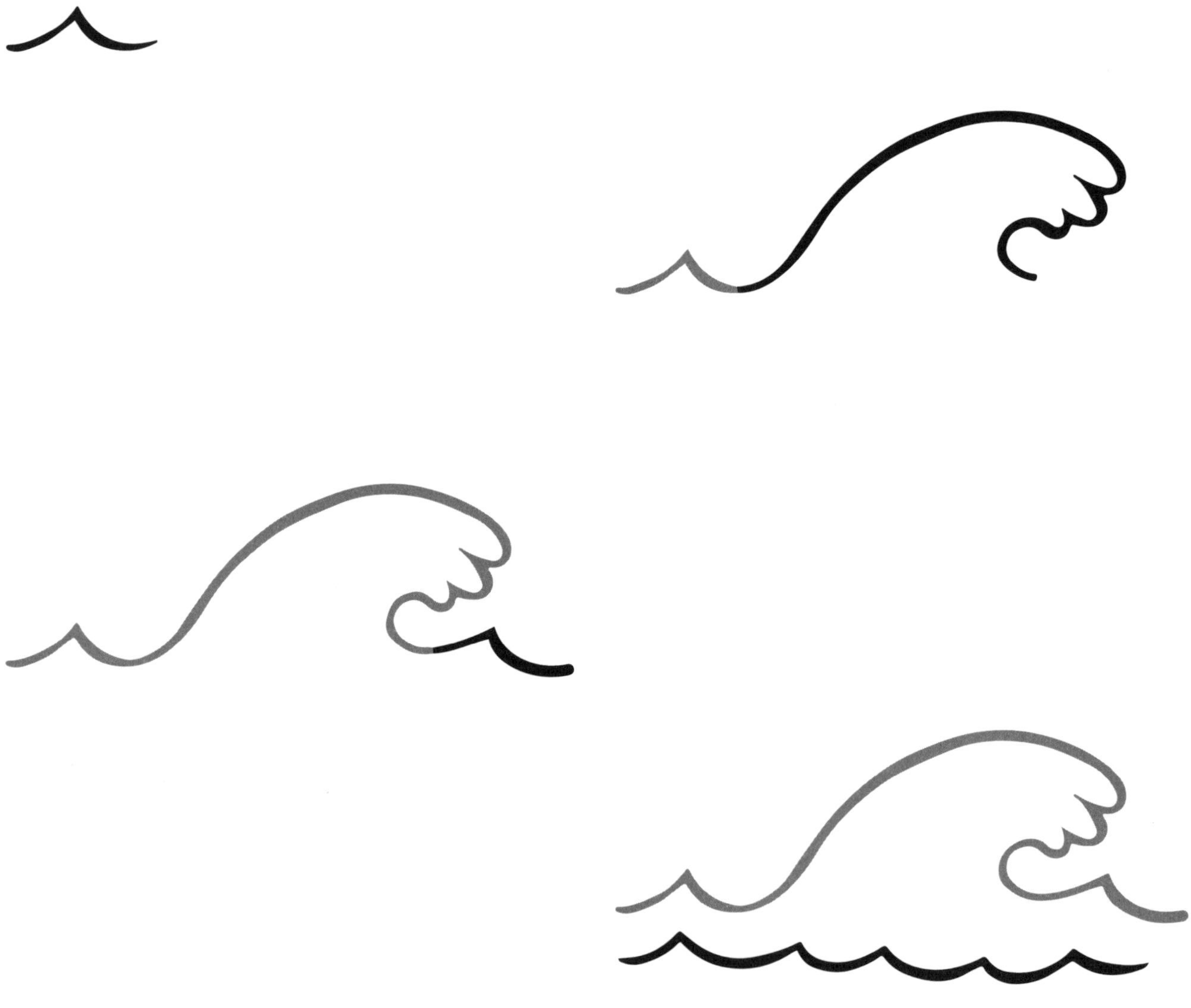

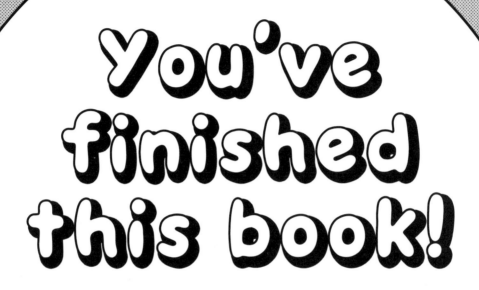

You've finished this book!

You can go back and practise
drawing the subjects again,
or make up your own.
Have fun drawing!